Lif[illegible] Atlantic Ocean

Ann Rossi

PEARSON

Boston, Massachusetts
Chandler, Arizona
Glenview, Illinois
Upper Saddle River, New Jersey

Photographs

Every effort has been made to secure permission and provide appropriate credit for photographic material. The publisher deeply regrets any omission and pledges to correct errors called to its attention in subsequent editions.

Unless otherwise acknowledged, all photographs are the property of Pearson Education, Inc.

Photo locators denoted as follows: Top (T), Center (C), Bottom (B), Left (L), Right (R), Background (Bkgd)

Opener: Medioimages/Photodisc/Thinkstock; 1 Medioimages/Photodisc/Thinkstock; 4 ©Wolfgang Kaehler/Corbis; 5 ©Kenneth McCray/SuperStock; 6 ©Morton Beebe/Corbis; 8 ©NASA; 10 ©Steve Vidler/SuperStock; 11 ©David Muench/Corbis; 12 ©Morton Beebe/Corbis; 13 ©Jeff Greenberg/The Image Works, Inc.; 15 ©Jeff Foott/Alamy.

ISBN-13: 978-0-328-67654-5
ISBN-10: 0-328-67654-3

1 2 3 4 5 6 7 8 9 10 V0FL 15 14 13 12 11

Florida's Atlantic Coastal Plain

Florida's Atlantic Coastal Plain lies along the east coast of Florida and ranges in width from about 30 to 100 miles (48 to 160 kilometers). As its name suggests, the Atlantic Coastal Plain borders the Atlantic Ocean. As a **plain**, it is low and flat.

Florida has about 580 miles (933 kilometers) of shoreline along the Atlantic coast. Some of Florida's largest cities lie along the Atlantic coast, which is generally more densely populated than Florida's inland areas.

The Atlantic Coastal Plain has **rural** areas as well as **urban** areas. Farmers grow crops and raise livestock, or farm animals, in some rural areas. Mining occurs in other rural areas. Some rural spaces remain undeveloped or are parks where people can enjoy the outdoors and discover the area's wildlife.

Florida's **climate** is warm and mild, but northern Florida has cooler winters than southern Florida. Come take a look at some of the places on Florida's Atlantic Coastal Plain.

Florida's Atlantic Coastal Plain is on the east coast of Florida and lies along the Atlantic Ocean.

St. Augustine and St. Johns County

Located in St. Johns County in northeastern Florida, St. Augustine is a small city lying just five feet above **sea level**. People from a variety of backgrounds live in St. Augustine, including many who were born in foreign countries.

St. Augustine is a city with a colorful past. Over hundreds of years, people have come to St. Augustine for many different reasons. Native Americans were the first to settle where St. Augustine stands today. Spain claimed Florida in 1513, and a Spanish explorer founded St. Augustine in 1565. St. Augustine is the oldest continuously occupied settlement established by Europeans in the present United States.

The narrow streets and houses with balconies in the old part of St. Augustine are reminders of the city's Spanish past.

In the late 1600s the Spanish built the Castillo de San Marcos (Cass-TEE-yo day san MAR-cos), to protect St. Augustine. Today, many visitors tour the fort.

At first, St. Augustine served as Spain's military headquarters in North America. In time St. Augustine grew into a city. By the 1870s many people came to St. Augustine from other parts of the United States for health reasons. They wanted to spend winters in its mild, dry climate. Soon businesspeople built hotels to attract healthy, wealthy tourists to St. Augustine.

Today, tourism continues to be an important business in St. Augustine. Tourism is the industry that serves people who travel for pleasure. About six million tourists from around the world visit St. Augustine each year. Many tourists come to St. Augustine to visit its historic sites, to golf, or to enjoy the nearby beaches and parks.

Like much of Florida, St. Augustine and the rest of St. Johns County have a mild climate. Summers are warmer and wetter than winters. The mild climate is ideal for farming. As a result, agriculture, or the planting of crops for food, is an important business in some rural areas. Farmers grow vegetables such as potatoes, cabbage, broccoli, and eggplant. Some people raise beef cattle.

Agriculture is an important business in St. Johns County, Florida.

This map shows some cities in Florida.

A mild climate and plentiful **resources** are two reasons that businesses are attracted to St. Johns County. Forests provide timber. Minerals and clay are mined in many rural parts of the northern Atlantic Coastal Plain.

Much of the coast around St. Augustine is a type of **limestone** called coquina (coh-KEE-nah). Coquina is found along Florida's Atlantic coast, from St. Augustine to Palm Beach, and is often used in building. Many structures in St. Augustine are built of coquina, including the Castillo de San Marcos.

Cape Canaveral and Surrounding Areas

Unlike St. Augustine, Cape Canaveral is a fairly young city. It has been a city only since the early 1960s. Like St. Augustine, Cape Canaveral is another small, low-lying city in Florida's Atlantic Coastal Plain. Bordered on the east by the Atlantic Ocean and on the west by the Banana River, Cape Canaveral is about halfway between Jacksonville and Miami. To the north of Cape Canaveral are Port Canaveral and the John F. Kennedy Space Center.

Goods are shipped from Port Canaveral to ports in the United States and other countries.

Facts About Cape Canaveral, Miami, and St. Augustine			
	Cape Canaveral	Miami	St. Augustine
Elevation (height above sea level)	9 feet	11 feet	5 feet
Land Area (square miles)	2.3	35.7	8.4
Population (year 2000)	8,829	362,470	11,592
Average Temperature In January	60.5°F	68.0°F	55.5°F
Average Temperature In July	81.8°F	82.5°F	80.8°F
Average Days With Precipitation In January	7	7	8
Average Days With Precipitation In July	16	16	14

Port Canaveral is an important port for cruise ships and for cargo ships. Some of the goods that pass through the port are cement, lumber, steel, minerals, petroleum, fresh fruits and vegetables, juice, and frozen foods.

Visitors enjoy touring the John F. Kennedy Space Center.

Many people come to Cape Canaveral because of its mild climate and ocean beaches. The mild climate also appealed to the United States government when it was deciding where to build the future John F. Kennedy Space Center, the place from which all space missions that carry crews are launched. The mild climate meant that the space center could operate year-round.

Natural spaces are important to the Cape Canaveral area in many ways. Tourists and residents alike enjoy the beaches in and around the city. The nearby Canaveral National Seashore is on a **barrier island** that includes ocean, beach, dune, **hammock**, lagoon, and salt marsh habitats. These habitats support several **endangered** species, such as the West Indian manatee and numerous kinds of migratory birds. Endangered loggerhead sea turtles nest on the sandy beach. An animal or plant is endangered when it is in danger of no longer existing. Behind the barrier island is Mosquito Lagoon, a valuable fishery for fish and shellfish.

Canaveral National Seashore has twenty-four miles of unsettled beach.

Many Haitians live in the bustling Caribbean community called Little Haiti. Visitors to Little Haiti may hear Creole spoken and can buy foods and other goods that are part of traditional Haitian life.

The Miami Area

Farther south along the Atlantic Coastal Plain is the city of Miami. With a population of more than 360,000, Miami is Florida's second largest city.

Due to its location, Miami has a tropical climate. Summers are wet and warm, or hot. Winters are warm, and frosts seldom occur.

People from all over the world live in Miami. In the year 2000, two-thirds of its residents were Hispanic. Many of them have a Cuban background. Miami's rich cultural traditions are reflected in many of its neighborhoods, such as Little Havana and Little Haiti.

Many Cubans came to the United States in the 1960s. Many of them settled in Miami in the neighborhood now known as Little Havana. They opened shops, parks, and restaurants that reflected the flavors and history of Cuba. Little Havana became the center of Miami's Cuban American community. Today, many residents from other parts of Latin America live in the area. Their cultural background is also reflected in the restaurants of Little Havana.

Cubans began coming to Miami in large numbers in the 1960s. Many new arrivals come first to Little Havana.

The Miami International Airport and the Port of Miami provide ways for people and goods to get into and out of Miami. Visitors to Miami include tourists, business travelers, and students. Many students come to the Miami area to attend college. The Port of Miami is known as the Cruise Capital of the World, but the port also ships goods around the world. The port provides more than ninety thousand jobs in the Miami-Dade County area.

Many resources in rural areas around Miami also provide jobs. Crops such as citrus and tropical fruits grow well in the rich soil and warm climate. Limestone and other materials are mined. However, development, or building on unsettled land, is causing some of the habitats that were once common in Miami-Dade County to disappear. For example, hammocks were once common as far north as Cape Canaveral. Now, only small patches remain in parts of the southern Atlantic Coastal Plain. Much of the Everglades has been drained for farmland.

The Everglades is the only place in the world where crocodiles and alligators live side by side.

Undeveloped rural areas are important. Many tourists come to southern Florida to see the wildlife and to visit parks such as Everglades National Park. The park has many kinds of plant communities, including mangrove and cypress swamps, hammocks, and saw grass prairies. Saw grass is a tall, grasslike plant with sharp, jagged edges. The Everglades are home to many plants, birds, and endangered animals, such as the American crocodile and West Indian manatee.

Care must be taken to preserve the varied resources of the Atlantic Coastal Plain, because it is those resources that make the region as popular and diverse as it is today.

Glossary

barrier island a long island that helps protect the mainland from pounding waves

climate the weather pattern of an area over a long period of time

endangered in danger of no longer existing

hammock a group of trees growing on a small, raised mound of land

limestone rock formed from a mineral in water or from shells and bones of certain sea animals

plain a large area of fairly low, flat land

resource a material that people use to meet their needs

rural having to do with the countryside

sea level the same height as the ocean

urban having to do with cities